MW01127165

This book belongs to

....

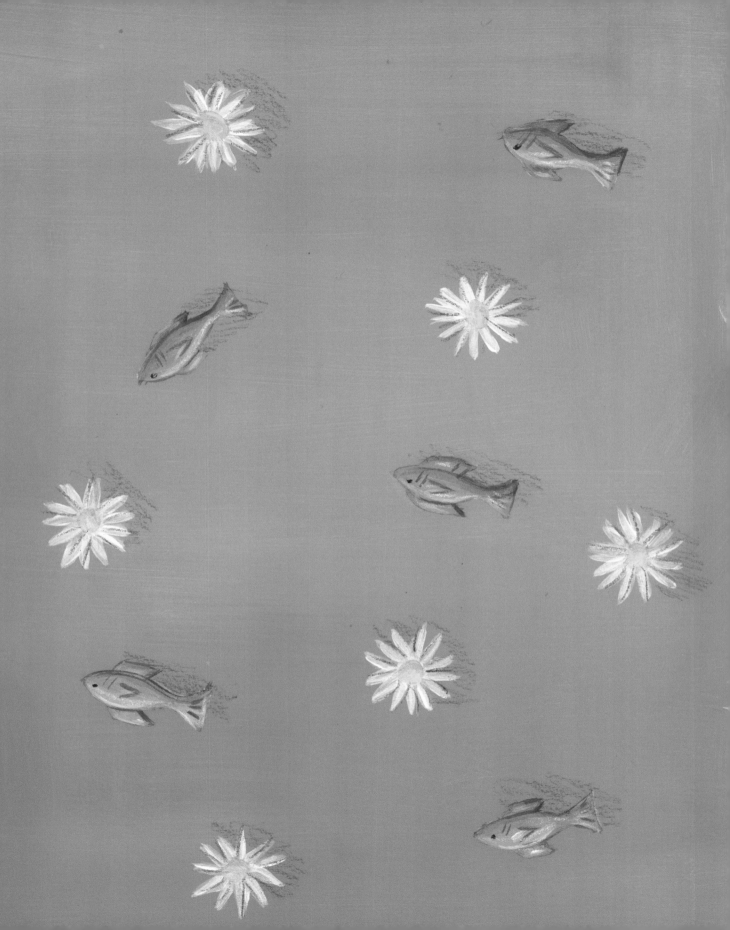

Thank you to my husband who always believed
this was possible when I had my doubts,
and my wonderful supportive children.

I am so grateful for so many things in my life,
especially my family and friends, new and old.

Diana

Published in Australia by
Books To Inspire Press
Perth, Western Australia
dianasmithbookstoinspire.com
author@dianasmithbookstoispire.com

First published in Australia in 2016
Text Copyright © Diana Smith 2016
Illustrations Copyright © Sarah Jane Marchant 2016

National Library of Australia Cataloguing in Publication entry

 NATIONAL LIBRARY OF AUSTRALIA   A catalogue record for this
book is available from the
National Library of Australia

ISBN: 978-0-6452072-2-4 (paperback)
ISBN: 978-0-6452072-4-8 (hardcover)

Illustrations by Sarah Jane Marchant
Book layout and typography by Sophie White
Printed by Ingram Spark

My Grateful Book

DIANA SMITH

Illustrated by Sarah Jane Marchant

It's the little things in life
That I don't want to miss

Like eyelashes that give
the people I love
A special butterfly kiss.

Water that we bathe in
Or drink and swim and fish.

Or rain running down the window,
Or collected in a dish.

Rainbows that show me colours
Blue, Yellow, red or green.

They are something I can never touch,
But awesome to be seen.

At the school I go to
with my friends,

The teachers are so great.

A B C D E

They help me learn
to read and write,

And I play with all my mates.

The beach is a place I like to go,
The sand, the surf, the sun.

Building sandcastles and collecting shells,
I always have lots of fun.

At home, I love my bedroom
It's where I can be alone
To read or listen to music
A place to call my own.

The food I'm given is very good
I try to eat my best.

The ones I love, they cook for me
And then I have a rest.

So as I close my eyes at night,
Filled with good things from today
I look forward to tomorrow
For more good things to come my way.

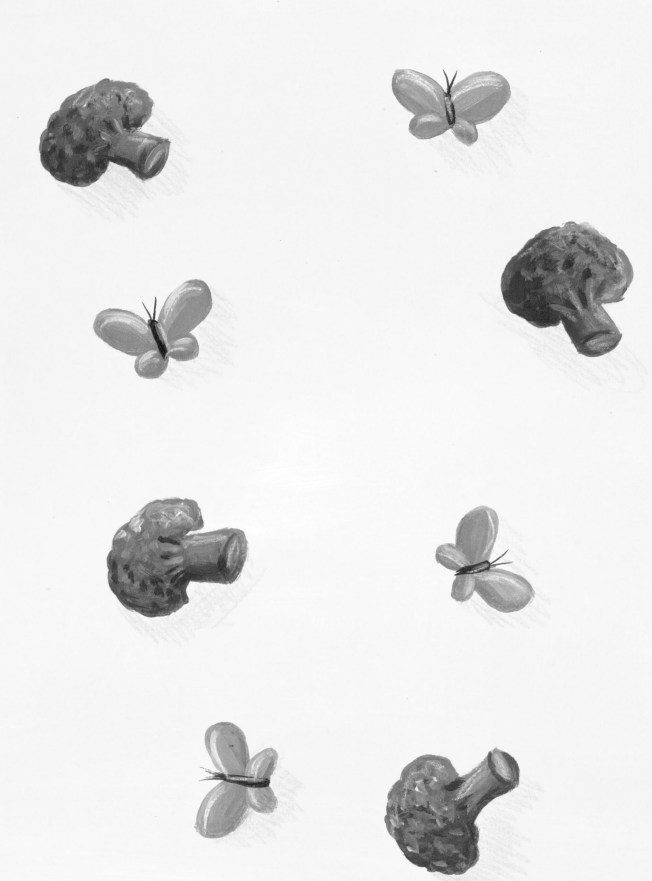

CPSIA information can be obtained
at www.ICGtesting.com
Printed in the USA
BVHW022235071121
621057BV00005B/22